ADVENTURES in THE MIDDLE AGES

Adventures? Are you joking?

We could get killed!

We could get really hungry, too.

Written by **Linda Bailey**
Illustrated by **Bill Slavin**

A & C Black • London

This book is for my daughter, Tess Grainger,
who loves travel and adventure every bit as much as I do.
L.B.

To Ted and Sue, who let me dress them in cardboard armour and
whack them with wooden swords when we were children.
B.S.

Acknowledgements

I am very grateful for the support of the B.C. Arts Council in the writing of this book. I would also like to express my gratitude to Dr Paul Dutton of Simon Fraser University and Dr Richard Unger of the University of British Columbia for reviewing my manuscript. Both were generous with their time and expertise, and any errors or inaccuracies in the text are my own.

A huge thank you to Valerie Wyatt, whose near mind-boggling skills as an editor gave my ideas a workable form. Thanks also to Bill Slavin for bringing the Binkertons so splendidly to life on the page and to Julia Naimska for her care with the book's design.

Through the many years of the Binkertons' evolution, my friend and fellow writer, Deborah Hodge, has been an unfailing source of insight and encouragement. Thanks, Debbie!
Thanks, too, to the first age-appropriate reader of the manuscript, Sarah Hunter.

My family, as always, provided a goofy, warm and enthusiastic environment in which to create, and I would like to thank Bill, Lia and Tess for their support. Last, but absolutely not least, I would like to thank Mr Visch of River-East-Collegiate-all-those-years-ago for first showing me that history could be fun. May all history students be so lucky!

This edition published 2000 in Great Britain by
A & C Black (Publishers) Ltd, 35 Bedford Row, London WC1R 4JH

First published 2000 in Canada by Kids Can Press Ltd

Edited by Valerie Wyatt
Designed by Julia Naimska
Printed in Hong Kong

ISBN 0-7136-5764-2

A CIP catalogue record for this book is available from the British Library.

Josh and Emma Binkerton stood in front of the Good Times Travel Agency, scared out of their wits.

Well, who wouldn't be scared? Good Times wasn't exactly an ordinary travel agency. It was as gloomy as a ghost, as grubby as a rubbish bin. Cobwebs drooped from the ceiling. Mouse droppings littered the floor. It looked as though no one had gone in or come out in twenty years!

But the Binkerton twins knew better. *They* had been inside before. *They* knew what kind of travel agency it really was.

3

Mr Pettigrew, the owner, was sitting exactly where he had sat the last time they visited.

4

Josh didn't care how creepy the place was. Ever since he could remember, he had dreamed about being a knight. To live in a castle, to wield a sword...

But Emma couldn't help remembering the last time they went time-travelling. They had taken their little sister, Libby, with them – and they had almost got themselves killed!

I want to go back to the Middle Ages and be a knight!

Oh dear! I'm glad we left Libby at home.

Mr Pettigrew quickly located the travel guidebook that would take them back through time.

Julian T. Pettigrew's Personal Guide to the MIDDLE AGES

The Middle Ages? Deary me. Could be dangerous.

Er... dangerous?

Just think, Emma. You'll be a princess!

to the MIDDLE AGES

Open this book and your journey's begun. Read every word and your journey is done.

Ignoring Emma's worries, Josh opened the guidebook. There was a terrible, wonderful flash, and...

Peasants are one of the groups, or classes, here in the Middle Ages. They're at the bottom of something called feudal society. Here is how it works.

All the land belongs to the king, but he grants most of it to powerful lords. In return, these lords promise to supply him with soldiers and to fight on his side in a war. They then grant some of their land to lesser lords or knights, who make the same kind of promise.

All the lords grant strips of land to peasants, who actually farm it. In return for their strips, the peasants have to work on the lord's land two or three days a week. They also have to pay to use the lord's mill and baking oven, and must give him eggs and hens and grain and... well, you get the picture.

The king rules. The lords and knights fight. The peasants work. Bad luck for the peasants.

9

Josh tried to explain who they *really* were...

... but the peasants weren't convinced.

Things went from bad to worse.

To Josh, the next step was obvious – find the nearest castle! It turned out to be a hard day's walk away. The Binkertons would have to wait until morning.

Fortunately, a kind peasant named Walter invited them to spend the night with his family. But first they'd have to earn their keep.

One more night, and I'll be a knight!

Dirt and drudgery!

Dawn to dusk!

Day after day!

I will never listen to Josh again, I will never listen to Josh again, I will –

A Peasant's Life

If you're looking for an easy life, do *not* become a peasant.

Farming in the Middle Ages involves endless hours of backbreaking work. Why? Well, except for a few oxen to pull the ploughs, it's all done by human muscle. There's very little fertiliser, so it's hard to grow a decent crop.

It's a tough life, and don't think you'll get off easy if you're a kid. In a peasant family, everybody works. The men do the heavy work in the fields, but women and children help out there, too. At planting time, women break up clods of soil with wooden mallets, while children scare birds away from the newly scattered seeds. Peasant women also cook, spin, weave, sew, garden and look after animals. Peasant children have their own chores, such as tending sheep and fetching water. They have plenty of time to work, because there's no school!

The peasants have to grow enough wheat, barley, oats, rye, peas and beans to feed themselves, their families and... everyone else.

The Binkertons worked as hard as horses, as hard as dogs, as hard as – well, peasants. When the day finally ended, they followed Walter home. His house turned out to be small. *Very* small.

I'm DESPERATE!
Where's the toilet?

A Peasant's House

Most peasants' houses are made of wattle and daub (branches woven together and covered with a mixture of mud and straw). They have dirt floors and roofs made of thatch or turf. The windows have shutters instead of glass.

A poor peasant's house may have only one room. It acts as the living room, bedroom and kitchen. Don't bother looking for the bathroom. There's no such thing. Without running water, a bath involves a lot of work, and most peasants don't get round to bathing very often. If you need to use the toilet, step outside. You may find a trench or a pit that someone has dug. If not, look for a bush to crouch behind, but please – make sure it's at least a stone's throw from the house.

Peasants sometimes have room-mates – large domestic animals such as cows and oxen that live inside the house. On a cold winter's night, these animals help to keep the house – and the peasants – warm. You might also spot smaller animals, such as rats and mice, living in the thatch. They don't *usually* fall on the people below.

The Binkerton kids tried hard to be polite – even though dinner was nothing but a chunk of bread and a bowl of mush.

Lovely hot pottage.

It looks... er, delicious.

Next time I'm bringing a sandwich!

A PEASANT'S FOOD

What do peasants eat? Not as much as they would like – especially in tough times! A peasant's main diet is coarse, dark bread and pottage (a soupy stew made with dried peas or beans and vegetables). A lucky peasant might have cheese or an egg and, sometimes, meat. An unlucky peasant – especially when crops are poor – may go to bed hungry.

Favourite peasant drinks are water, cider, water, ale (beer) and, of course, water.

As soon as it got dark, the whole family went to bed. That's when the Binkertons found out that Walter's house was a little short on beds.

Itchy clothes.

It's not the clothes, Libby. Clothes don't bite!

Forget it! Bed's full.

A Peasant's Furniture

There's usually not much: a table, a bench, a few stools, a wooden chest or two and a straw mattress to sleep on. Looking for a lamp? Not a chance. Even candles are expensive for most peasants. When darkness falls, it's time for bed.

Bed, unfortunately, often means fleas and lice. Both are extremely common in the Middle Ages and hard to get rid of. Rich or poor, everyone itches. You will simply have to get used to it.

If you think it's easy to sleep seven-to-a-bed when you're being bitten by fleas and lice, you can think again. It was a *very* long night.

15

When the Binkertons got up the next morning, they were surprised to discover that the village was having a fair. They had planned to set out for the castle immediately, but no Binkerton has *ever* been able to resist a party.

HOLY AND MARKET DAYS

Holy days, or feast days, are special days when people rest from work and go to church, usually to honour saints. Afterwards, they get the day off to enjoy themselves. Peasants in the Middle Ages love a celebration. With their hard lives, who can blame them?

Sometimes markets and fairs are held on feast days. If you have anything you want to sell, here's your chance. You might also get to see travelling entertainers – acrobats, musicians, animal trainers, jugglers or puppeteers. You can play games and sports or watch contests. You can even dance or wrestle in the churchyard – as long as you don't mind the priest glaring at you.

The priest, by the way, is a pretty important person. Almost everyone here is a Christian, and the Church has a lot of power. It also has a lot of wealth. The peasants give one-tenth of everything they produce to the Church. This is called the tithe.

P.S. You may come across a nasty sport in which vicious dogs are set loose on a tied-up bear. It's called bear-baiting. It was very popular in the Middle Ages, but I suggest you avoid it!

Things were definitely looking up for the Binkertons. They were having an excellent time... until Josh became a little too talkative.

A crowd gathered. Off to one side stood a sinister red-bearded stranger. Unfortunately, the only one to notice him was Libby.

The Earth travels around the Sun.

It's called electricity. You flick a switch and light comes on.

Disease is caused by tiny creatures called germs.

Are you mad, boy?

What an imagination!

?

WHAT PEOPLE BELIEVE

Here in the Middle Ages, people have some interesting ideas about the world and how it works:

- The Earth is the centre of the universe. The stars and Sun revolve around it.
- Disease is caused by bad vapours.
- One way to cure ill people is to bleed them (cut open a vein and let blood drip out). Another way is to attach blood-sucking leeches to their bodies.
- Foreign lands are home to strange creatures – one-eyed giants, dog-headed people and men with the bodies of horses.

Suddenly, a hush fell over the crowd. Josh looked up to see a group of finely dressed men on horses.

CLOTHING IN THE MIDDLE AGES

You can tell people's rank by the clothing they wear.

Peasant clothes are made of rough, home-spun linen or wool. Peasant women wear long, loose gowns. The men wear tunics (knee-length tops) over short trousers called breeches. Both wear woollen hose (stockings) and belts. Peasants have few clothes, and they wear them for years and years. You would too if you had to spin, weave and sew every garment by hand.

Clothing worn by noble people is finer, richer and brighter than peasants' clothes. Both men and women wear tunics fastened with brooches or chains, and cloaks over the top when it's cold. Nobles' clothes are made of wool, silk or linen. Often they are trimmed or lined with fur, or decorated with jewels. They cost so much that, like peasants' clothes, they are worn year after year. They're even handed on to relatives after death!

Josh was thrilled to receive a personal invitation to the castle. The Binkertons set off at once.

At the edge of the woods, they came across peasants gathering firewood. But the deeper they travelled into the forest, the darker and the more silent it became.

Suddenly there was a huge crash! Two peasants charged out of the woods, carrying animals they had poached.

Right behind the fleeing peasants came a young woman on horseback.

Are these the poachers?

No, ma'am, we haven't had an egg in days.

Not that kind of poacher, Josh.

When Josh asked the young woman for directions to the castle, he discovered that she *lived* there! She was Sir Richard's wife, Lady Margaret, out on a hunt.

Can I see your pet bird?

Once they had directions, the Binkertons started walking again... and walking... and walking. To make things worse, it started to rain.

They should call it the Mud-dle Ages.

I bet this never happened to Sir Lancelot.

THE FOREST

The forests belong to the king and the lords, who are the only people allowed to hunt there. They use hounds to hunt deer and boars. But their favourite kind of hunting is hawking – using a trained falcon to catch and kill smaller birds. Good hunting hawks are valuable and are treated very well by their owners, who carry them around on their wrists, even in church and at meals.

At certain times, peasants are allowed into the forest to collect firewood and feed acorns to their pigs, but only with the permission of you-know-who.

Hunting in the forest without permission is called poaching. Don't try it! Poachers can be imprisoned or lose an eye or a hand. They can even be executed.

21

A MEDIEVAL CASTLE

Welcome to your very first castle! What's it for, anyway?

A castle is a fortress that protects a lord against his enemies. Castles are often built at river crossings, in mountain passes or on islands. The best spot is somewhere high, steep and easy to defend. Castles have:

- stone walls that may be 6 metres thick or more;
- a water-filled moat (ditch) to keep out attackers;
- a drawbridge that can be pulled up if the castle is attacked;
- a gatehouse where the castle's soldiers stand guard;
- high towers where lookouts keep watch.

A castle is a home to the lord, his family and their servants, soldiers and guests. There might be hundreds of people who live, work, eat, sleep and play here, quite close together. Privacy? In the Middle Ages, forget it!

A castle is a headquarters for the area. All sorts of business goes on here to do with the lord's lands and the people who work on them. Criminals are sometimes tried in the castle, and important documents are kept here. In times of war, people living in local villages come to the castle for protection.

To Josh's horror, he was rushed into Sir Richard's presence by large soldiers, who called him a 'fool'. That's when Josh realised the truth. He hadn't been invited to the castle to become a knight after all. Sir Richard had mistaken him for a jester!

THE GREAT HALL

The most important room in a castle is the Great Hall. This is where the lord has meetings and looks after the business of running his estates. People eat here, too. Some even sleep here.

ENTERTAINMENT
People in a castle like to be entertained. Minstrels sing long story-songs. Musicians, jugglers, acrobats and actors also take their turn. For laughs, there's the jester (also called the fool, or buffoon), who dresses in a brightly coloured outfit and tells rude or funny stories. Sometimes he waves a pig's bladder filled with dried peas. If you see a jester doing this, pretend you think it's funny.

GAMES
Board games such as chess, draughts and backgammon are popular here in the Middle Ages. (If you want to play Monopoly, unfortunately you'll have to wait a few centuries.)

Josh was positive he and his sisters were going to be hurled into the dungeon. It turned out, however, that the castle kitchen was short of workers.

You said I'd be a princess.

Who is that guy, anyway?

A CASTLE KITCHEN

Vegetarians may want to give the castle kitchen a miss. A speciality of the house is large hunks of meat – beef, pork, mutton (sheep), game – roasted on a spit over an open fire. To make sure the meat cooks evenly, a scullion (servant boy) turns the spit. This is hard, hot, heavy work. Do *not* volunteer.

Soups and stews are cooked in large iron cauldrons hung over the fire.

If you'd like to try baking bread, start by building a fire in the oven. Leave it to burn until there is only hot coal. Then scrape out all the ashes. Put bread dough in the oven and close the door. The leftover heat will bake the bread.

With all these fires, there's always the risk of an accident. That's why castle kitchens are usually in a separate building in the courtyard, away from the main castle.

The next day, Sir Richard and Lady Margaret had important guests, so the Binkertons got a peek at a castle feast.

Hmmm... plates you can eat.

Peacocks? Seagulls? Do you really eat this stuff?

A CASTLE MEAL

At meal times, long tables are put up in the Great Hall. The lord has his own table, on a raised platform – just in case anyone isn't *sure* who's in charge.

What does a lord eat? Plenty! The same goes for his family and friends, especially at a feast.

Noble people eat a lot of meat – venison (deer), pork, rabbit, mutton – served with rich, spicy sauces. They enjoy fish, too, and poultry – goose, duck and chicken, plus 'odd birds' such as peacocks, vultures, blackbirds, seagulls and swans. Puddings, cheese, nuts and dried fruit are also on the menu. Vegetables? They're not very important.

Table manners here are a little... unusual. Forks aren't used much, so make do with a knife and your fingers. (Most people carry their own knife in a sheath at their waist.) Bowls and cups are shared – unless you're the lord, of course. The plates (called trenchers) are just large slices of stale bread.

Feel free to toss your leftovers to the dogs. That's why they're there.

Sleeping in a castle turned out to be not much better than sleeping in a peasant's cottage. Emma barely slept at all. She was too busy trying to get through the guidebook – and back to her real life!

Fleas here, too?

I'd give my right arm for a torch.

SLEEPING IN A CASTLE

The lord and his family have their own bedroom with a big, fancy, curtained bed, and there may also be a few other private sleeping chambers in a castle.

But most people in the household just sleep wherever they can – on straw mattresses, on benches or chests, or even just on the rushes or straw scattered on the castle floors. Some spots, especially around the hearth, can get a little crowded. But look on the bright side – crowding together helps to keep you warm. There's nothing quite as cold, damp and draughty as a medieval castle.

Emma also tried to sneak in some reading time at work. But the guidebook was attracting the wrong kind of attention.

A servant with a book?!

She must have stolen it.

It says here that books are valuable. Wait a minute... Oh no! He's after the guidebook.

I tried to warn her.

Could it be true? Was the red-bearded stranger really trying to steal the guidebook? This was scary. The guidebook was the Binkertons' only way to get home. Emma realised that they'd have to be much more careful in future.

READING, WRITING AND BOOKS

Most people in the Middle Ages can't read. Just as well – there aren't that many books anyway. Paper (invented in China) isn't commonly used in Europe yet, so they have to use parchment (dried sheepskin) or vellum (dried calfskin) instead. The printing press hasn't been invented either, so books have to be copied one at a time with a goose quill and ink. Afterwards, they're decorated, often with real gold or silver.

Are you getting the picture? Books are rare and valuable here. Sometimes they're even chained to their cases in libraries. If you have any with you, for goodness' sake, hang on to them!

The guidebook wasn't their only problem. Emma was getting *extremely* tired of plucking poultry, and Josh was still no closer to becoming a knight.

But their biggest problem was Libby. The littlest Binkerton seemed to be everywhere at once! Josh and Emma were going crazy trying to keep up with her.

Still, Libby did manage to make an important friend – Lady Margaret. When Sir Richard went off to visit the king, Libby and the lady became constant companions.

INSIDE A CASTLE

If you have a chance, make sure you take a complete tour of a castle. Start with the bailey (the castle courtyard, inside the outer walls). This area can be as crowded and busy as a small town. There may even be more than one bailey. See if you can find:

1. A barn
2. A kitchen
3. Kennels
4. A laundry
5. A vegetable garden
6. A well to provide fresh water
7. Workshops (for carpenters, blacksmiths and other craftsmen)
8. Stables

30

Also do a tour of the castle keep (the main inner building). This stronghold is the last place of retreat in a battle. Often it's the lord's residence as well. Look for the following:

9. A solar (private rooms for the lord and his family)

10. Garderobes (toilets)
11. The Great Hall (sometimes a separate building)
12. A guard room for soldiers
13. A chapel (small church)
14. A storage area for food, weapons and ammunition
15. A dungeon for prisoners

The day after Sir Richard left, Josh finally got a lucky break. He was transferred from the kitchen to the stables.

Stables? Horses! Knights!

I'll be middle-aged myself before I become a knight.

Stable work was dirty – and smelly – but at least Josh got to meet some knights. He also saw squires not much older than himself, and young boys who were still pages.

Knight school! Now this is more like it.

Looking around the stables, Josh discovered some very old armour... and an even older horse. It took him forever to put the armour on. And then he had to dress his horse!

No, really. You look terrific.

Finally, he was ready – Sir Josh!

Stand back! I could be dangerous.

KNIGHTS AND THEIR CODE

No day in the Middle Ages is complete without a knight!
Knights are armoured soldiers on horseback. They live by a set of unwritten rules called the code of chivalry. This means that a knight is supposed to be loyal, brave, courteous, merciful, truthful, gentle, kind, generous, humble, true and protective of the weak and poor. Unfortunately, knights don't always obey the rules. Some loot and rob. Others kill their enemies – and even innocent bystanders – without blinking an eye.

HOW TO DRESS LIKE A KNIGHT
Relax. Armour isn't nearly as uncomfortable as it looks. Okay, it's heavy, but it's also flexible with clever joints for free movement.
Start with your chain-mail stockings (chausses), which include chain-mail feet. (Chain mail is made of linked iron rings).

Add your padded jacket (aketon). Next, put on your coat of chain mail (hauberk). Notice the special chain-mail mittens (mufflers) for your hands. Add a surcoat on top to protect you from the rain. Don't forget your helmet!
Getting a little warm in there? Try to stay out of the sun. It's not unknown for knights in armour to die of heatstroke.

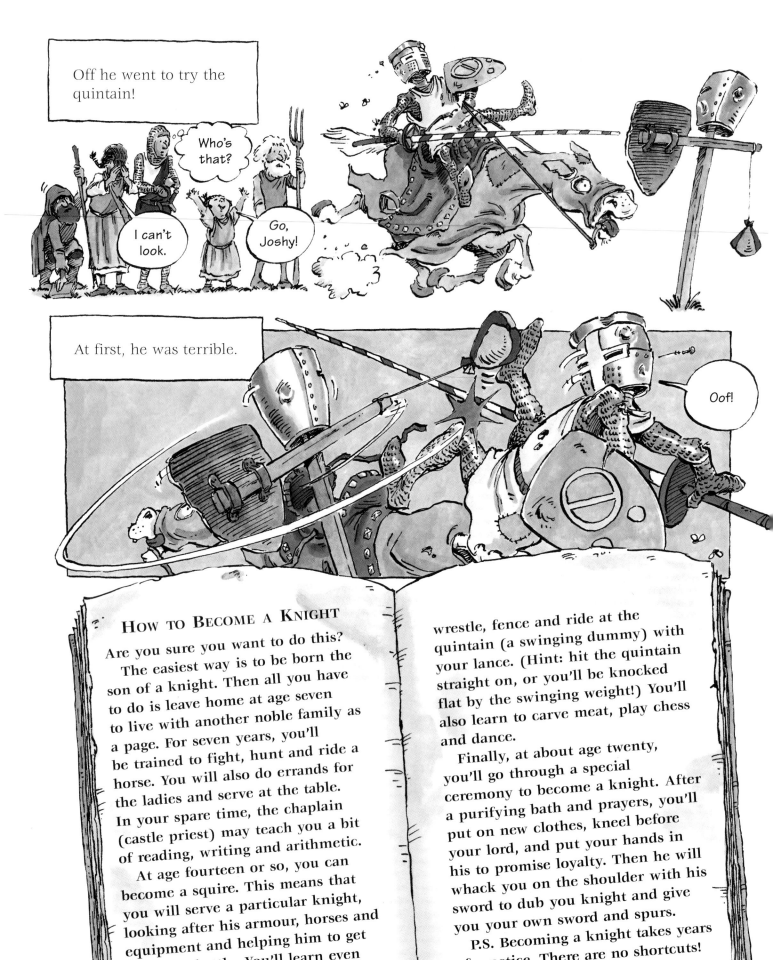

Off he went to try the quintain!

Who's that?

I can't look.

Go, Joshy!

At first, he was terrible.

Oof!

How to Become a Knight

Are you sure you want to do this? The easiest way is to be born the son of a knight. Then all you have to do is leave home at age seven to live with another noble family as a page. For seven years, you'll be trained to fight, hunt and ride a horse. You will also do errands for the ladies and serve at the table. In your spare time, the chaplain (castle priest) may teach you a bit of reading, writing and arithmetic.

At age fourteen or so, you can become a squire. This means that you will serve a particular knight, looking after his armour, horses and equipment and helping him to get ready for battle. You'll learn even more about fighting, hunting and riding. You'll run, shoot arrows, wrestle, fence and ride at the quintain (a swinging dummy) with your lance. (Hint: hit the quintain straight on, or you'll be knocked flat by the swinging weight!) You'll also learn to carve meat, play chess and dance.

Finally, at about age twenty, you'll go through a special ceremony to become a knight. After a purifying bath and prayers, you'll put on new clothes, kneel before your lord, and put your hands in his to promise loyalty. Then he will whack you on the shoulder with his sword to dub you knight and give you your own sword and spurs.

P.S. Becoming a knight takes years of practice. There are no shortcuts! Don't even think about it!

But after he had tried it eight or ten times, he was...

Whoooa!

...even worse.

Aaaaagh!

It was very discouraging.

Hopeless! I'll never be a knight.

Josh staggered to his feet, expecting to be dragged away by large, angry knights. But looking around, he was surprised to find that he was all alone.

Where's everybody gone?

Most of the castle's inhabitants were gathered at the main gate, staring out at a strange sight. Frightened peasants were hurrying into the castle, shouting the news – the castle was about to be attacked!

36

With Sir Richard away, Lady Margaret quickly took charge. She summoned all the fighting men in the castle and gave them orders for the castle's defence.

THE CASTLE AT WAR

Stuck in a castle that's under attack? Don't panic. Remember, castles are designed to protect the people inside. Here's how:

1. The wall-walk has plenty of space for castle soldiers to stand and fight.
2. The machicolations (projecting parts of castle walls) have holes through which stones and hot liquids can be dropped.
3. A portcullis (iron door) slides down to keep attackers out.
4. The gatehouse has 'murder holes' through which boiling water, oil or rocks can be dropped on to attackers.
5. The castle keep is the final inner stronghold where defenders can hide if the outer walls are breached.
6. The murderesses (special slits in castle walls, wide on the inside but narrow on the outside) let arrows out but not in.
7. The crenellated battlements (walls with toothlike structures on top) allow castle soldiers to fight and hide at the same time.
8. The tall towers are perfect for shooting arrows from.

On a different side of the castle is a sally port (small door) that allows defending soldiers to sneak out and do damage to the enemy.

The Binkertons watched nervously as Sir William's army surrounded the castle. In the days that followed, they got even *more* nervous as enemy soldiers tried to force their way inside.

Hmmm... What manner of strange book is this?

How to Attack a Castle

- Try to batter down the main gate with your battering ram. (Hint: check first to see whether the drawbridge has been pulled up. If so, it is EXTREMELY IMPORTANT to fill in the moat with dirt and logs *before* you start battering.)
- Use a scaling ladder to climb over the castle walls. Or push an assault tower (a large tower on wheels) up to the walls and try to get inside that way. Make sure the moat is filled in first. (See above.)

- Hurl nasty things over the castle walls. Large rocks are good. So are giant flaming arrows. Dead rotting animals are terrific.
- Dig a miner's tunnel and build a fire under the castle wall. If you're lucky, the fire will 'undermine' the foundations and bring the wall down.
- When all else fails, try sneaking in. Dress up in peasants' clothes or women's clothes – or both. Take gifts with you.

Let us in. We're peasants, bringing food.

Yeah, right! And I'm the King!

How to Defend a Castle

- Before you do anything else, PULL UP THE DRAWBRIDGE! If your enemies are trying to batter down the castle gate, drop things on them. Pots of fire, large rocks, quicklime, boiling water – use anything that's handy.
- Hide inside the towers or behind the castle battlements. Fire arrows and rocks down at the enemy.
- Use forked sticks to push scaling ladders off the walls. If you see a wooden tower getting close, shoot flaming arrows at it.
- Watch out for underground miners. Stand basins filled with lead pellets or water on your castle walls. If the pellets or water jiggle, you'll know that digging is going on down below.
- Watch out for enemies in disguise! Trust no one!

Watching the battle, the Binkertons were astounded – especially Josh. These knights were not nearly as noble, fine and chivalrous as he had imagined.

Those guys out there are hurling dead cows at us!

Well, the ones in here are pouring boiling water on people's heads!

Finally, the flaming arrows and flying cows slackened off. The Binkertons were relieved – until they found out that a castle's attackers could win simply by doing... nothing. Sir William had the castle surrounded. Nobody could get out – and no food could get in.

It's a siege. When our food is gone, we'll have to eat rats and grass.

Rats?

Grass?

That did it! The Binkertons had seen all they wanted to see of the Middle Ages.

Right, I've had enough of this! Give me the guidebook.

What? I thought you had it.

But where was the guidebook? In the excitement of the attack, the Binkertons had hardly given it a thought. Suddenly they remembered the red-bearded stranger.

Oh no! The stranger gone? With their guidebook? But without it, the Binkertons couldn't go home. There was only one thing left to do. Panic!

Where is that weirdo?

The stranger? He was a spy. He ran off to join the enemy!

We're trapped here!

We'll starve to death!

I'm *already* starving!

Fortunately, the Binkertons were not the kind of kids to lie down and starve without a fight. Emma saw a way to get the guidebook back *and* save the castle. But her plan would take nerves of steel, as well as speed and agility. It would take – a knight in shining armour!

But you're not listening. I failed knight school!

What do you think? Does this look like Sir William's coat of arms?

When Josh was ready, Emma sent him out through the sally port – right into the heart of enemy territory! Within seconds, he had everyone's attention.

You must be... er, Sir William of Wolfenstow, right?

Help!

?!

While Josh kept Sir William's men busy, Emma and Libby sneaked up on the enemy's supply carts.

Emma's plan worked! But then she and Libby had to run for their lives!

The girls had thrown the enemy camp into total chaos. This gave Josh his chance! He found the stranger...

CHAAAAAAARGE!

captured the guidebook...

... and raced back to the castle.

Gaaangwaaaaay!

The Binkertons had saved the day!

Joshy, look!

How can I ever thank you?

All in a day's — I mean, knight's — work.

Home!

The Binkertons had had more than enough excitement for one holiday. Emma was right. It was time to go home. Turning to the end of the guidebook, they read the last few pages, closed the book and...

The Binkertons were so eager to see their parents that they hurried off with barely a goodbye.

Emma swore she would *never* go near the travel agency again.

But never? Well, that's a very long time.

Even for time-travellers.

THE MIDDLE AGES

Fact or fantasy?

How much can you believe of *Adventures in the Middle Ages?* The story of the Binkertons and their adventures is just that – a story. However, all the information in *Julian T. Pettigrew's Personal Guide to the Middle Ages* is based on things that we know really happened in the Middle Ages – in other words, historical fact.

More about the Middle Ages

Middle of what, you ask? Excellent question! The Middle Ages is the name given to the 1000-year period in Europe between (approximately) 500 and 1500 AD. It's called 'middle' because it came between an 'ancient' age and a more 'modern' age. The ancient age was the time of the Greek and Roman civilisations. The more modern age began after 1500 with a new interest in learning and the arts, the formation of larger countries and the growth of trade and exploration. Sometimes the word 'medieval' is used to describe people, things and ideas in the Middle Ages. It comes from *medium aevium* (Latin for 'middle age').

The red section of the map shows the part of the world that makes up Europe today. It stretches from Ireland and Portugal all the way to Russia, and includes more than thirty countries. In the Middle Ages, many of these countries had not yet formed. Others were just beginning to develop.

The Binkertons' story is set in the High Middle Ages of the twelfth or thirteenth centuries. These were the peak years of castle-building. Guns and cannons were not yet used in warfare, so castles were the best defence against attacking forces.

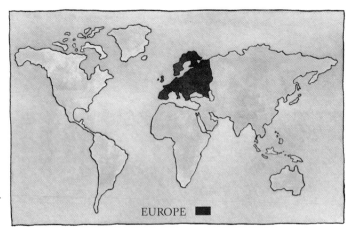

EUROPE ■

Another good defence was to have a force of armed soldiers on horseback – in other words, knights. But lords in castles and knights on horseback get hungry and, as the Binkertons found out, the people who provided the food and did most of the other work were the peasants, toiling away on their farms. Peasants, knights and lords were all bound to one another by ties of loyalty and duty. For a long time, these ties held this 'feudal' society together and kept life more or less the same.

Medieval people were also united by their religious beliefs. Nearly everyone in Europe during the Middle Ages was a Roman Catholic. People's beliefs helped them to accept their situation in this life because they could look forward to a better life after they died.

But change was coming. Even though power and wealth were still mostly in the hands of the nobles and the Church, towns were beginning to grow. They were centres of trade and home to a newly emerging 'middle' class of merchants and craftspeople. Many town activities were organised by guilds (associations of workers which regulated products and prices, standards and training).

Other changes were coming, too. Later in the Middle Ages, famine and disease (namely the Black Death or bubonic plague) would wipe out millions of people. Many of the peasants who survived would go to work in the towns where they could earn more money. The towns would grow even bigger. There would be changes to warfare, too. New weapons such as cannons would mean that castles were no longer useful defences – but wait a minute! This sounds like a completely different story...